Spec...
learning about and learning from religious festivals

Special times in religions are those set apart to celebrate, remember and give thanks for events and experiences which have defined the beliefs and practices of a faith. Some are sombre days of fasting and repentance, others are days of rejoicing – the feast days or festivals.

Festivals are a popular aspect of primary RE. We enjoy them because they have good stories and lots of colourful activities children can get involved in. But they are much more than this. They provide a wonderful 'window' into the beliefs, values, hopes and commitments of faith communities. As such, it is essential that we give children the means and opportunity to explore these aspects. If we only touch on the externals – the foods, the traditions and the stories – without getting inside the real meaning and purpose of the festival, we fall into the trap of letting the means become the end. Let's get festivals-based RE teaching beyond 'retelling the story' and look for some reasons why festivals work, matter and are the favourite bit of faith in many traditions.

Joyce Mackley
Editor

Things to note...

Many of the activities in this book complement QCA RE schemes of work:

1E How do Jewish people express their beliefs in practice? (Section 4: What is the festival of Passover?)

2C Celebrations (generic)

3B How and why do Hindus celebrate Divali?

4C Why is Easter important to Christians?

5B How do Muslims express their beliefs through practices?

For details, see www. standards.dfes.gov. uk/schemes2/religion/ ?view=get

Contents

Teaching religious festivals: some tips for teachers

Why teach festivals?

Because they are...

- outward manifestations of religious faith;
- shared experiences;
- expressions of the human need to have 'high days' and 'holidays', to celebrate things of significance and value in our lives;
- celebrations of personal (birthdays or anniversaries) and community (jubilees or anniversaries) identity. The marking of events which say something about who we are and what matters to us.

What *do* we need to remember and avoid?

- Avoid only looking at the external features, the things people do and say or eat.
- Explore *why* people keep special days and times of year. As teachers, we always need to keep in mind the question: 'What do we want pupils to learn from religious festivals?' The chart below identifies some important aspects and some examples from three religions.

What's in a festival? A shared experience

Shared memories

Remembering past events:

Passover: the night the people of Israel escaped slavery;

Easter: the death and resurrection of Jesus;

Id-ul-Adha: Ibrahim's preparedness to sacrifice his son.

Shared beliefs

A living expression of beliefs:

Passover: God's power to deliver his people;

Easter: God becoming human and dying on the cross to bring forgiveness and a new beginning;

Id-ul-Adha: obedience and commitment to the will of Allah.

Shared values

Festivals are ways of passing on the beliefs and values which matter most to a community.

Shared hopes

Expressing hope for the future:

Passover: that once again the Jewish people will be freed from oppression;

Easter: the promise of new life beyond death;

Id-ul-Adha: Ummah – a worldwide fellowship of Muslims based on sharing and equality.

Shared commitments

That people's faith will be renewed:

Passover: that Jewish people will work for justice and freedom from oppression;

Easter: working for 'life before death' for all those in need;

Id-ul-Adha: to overcome temptation and evil and do Allah's will.

Mind-mapping special times

For the teacher

Mind-mapping is a strategy which can be used with students as young as 4 and as old as 94!

It is a visual way of organising and remembering thoughts and information, first devised by Tony Buzan (**www.mind-map.com**).

It is useful for...

- providing a visual picture of ideas, words or learning;
- finding out what pupils know at the start of an activity (assessing prior knowledge);
- giving children the opportunity to explore information using different intelligences;
- assessing the amount of learning that has occurred at the end of a topic.

Try using a mind-map to provide an overview of a unit. Frequent reference to it will support visual and logical-mathematical learners – both pupils and teachers!

This is a mind-map produced by a 10-year-old at the end of a unit exploring Peter's experiences of Holy Week. It shows evidence of very good achievement – not only of knowledge and understanding of the main events, but a sensitive awareness and insight into the personal experiences of Peter.

How do you mind-map? A step-by-step guide

1 Identify the topic.

2 Brainstorm the ideas, and the child writes or draws key words or pictures (or someone scribes their ideas).

3 Sort the words and/or pictures into groups or categories.

4 Underline or circle all those in the same group with the same colour.

5 On a large sheet of paper, draw a picture or write the title of the topic in the centre.

6 Choose one group of ideas and, using the colour of this group, draw a branch. Write the category heading inside or along the branch.

7 For each idea in the category, draw a sub-branch and draw a picture or write some words.

8. Repeat for each group or category of words – building up a series of branches around the central topic.

See also...

Interactive *Kidspiration* software for younger pupils, supporting this kind of visual learning: www.inspiration.com

Special Sundays
A mind-mapping activity for younger pupils

For the teacher

Before doing the following activity, children will have explored why Sunday is a special day for Christians. They will know that it is a weekly reminder of the day when Jesus came alive again on the first Easter Sunday. They will have heard how Christians often meet together for worship on this special day and they will have talked about the good things about having special days to say thank you, to celebrate and to be with family and friends.

This activity could be used both as a starter and as a follow-up to learning. When used with clear assessment criteria it can provide evidence of pupil achievement. Children who might struggle with the mind-map could sort the picture cards into groups such as Palm Sunday, Easter Sunday, Christian Sunday and My Sunday, explaining their ideas as they do so.

Pictures to support learning: copy and cut out.
Children could select from these to add to their brainstorm and mind-map, or draw their own.

Key word: Sunday

→ Brainstorm: ask the child to write down, draw or tell an adult things they associate with Sunday.
If needed, the adult could suggest some triggers such as: *What do you like about Sunday? What do you know about Sunday? Why is Sunday a special day for people who follow Jesus? What do many Christians do on Sundays? What happened to Jesus on Easter Sunday?*

→ Ask the child to sort the brainstorm into groups or categories of ideas by underlining everything in the same group with the same colour.

→ Make a mind-map. Ask the child to draw a picture for Sunday in the middle of a large piece of paper and then to draw different coloured lines out from the picture – the same colours as those used in the sorting activity. Along each line they then draw pictures and write words to represent all the ideas in that category.

Easter
Developing the theme across the primary school

For the teacher

- Easter is the most important festival for all Christians. Many primary schools teach about Easter annually. If you take this approach, careful planning to increase challenge and to help children build on earlier learning is very important.

- Below, you can see a suggested pattern of progression. Activities for some of the themes suggested here are outlined on pages 6 to 12. Others can be found in earlier publications in this series, as indicated in the grid.

Fact file: Easter

- Easter celebrates the resurrection of Jesus from the dead.

- The Easter festival celebrates events of the last week of Jesus' life, known as Holy Week. It begins on Palm Sunday, the day Jesus arrived in Jerusalem, and ends on Easter Sunday, a day of joy celebrating the resurrection of Jesus after his death on the cross on Good Friday.

- The cross is the main symbol of Christianity. The crucifix emphasises Jesus' suffering for humanity; the plain cross emphasises the resurrection.

Year	Theme	Learning about Easter	Learning from Easter	Activities
R	New life	Easter eggs	Signs of spring New beginnings	Pages 6–7
1	Celebration	Easter Sunday Sundays	Times of joy and celebration	Pages 4 and 6
2	Easter garden	Outline of main events of Easter story with a focus on events in the garden	New beginnings – bulbs, seeds – all look dead but hold the promise of new life – resurrection	Page 8
3	Sorrow/joy	Good Friday/Easter Sunday	Sad and happy times	See *Developing Primary RE: Jesus* pages 24–29
4	Service to others	Last Supper Jesus washes the feet of the disciples	How can we show humility? How can we 'serve' others?	Pages 9–10 See also *Developing Primary RE: Jesus* pages 24–26
5	Failure and forgiveness	Peter's story – events of the last week through Peter's eyes	Times we have let someone down; being given a second chance; making amends.	Page 3 See also *Developing Primary RE: Faith Stories* page 17
6	New beginnings	An ending becomes a new beginning Jesus' death and resurrection (Eastern Orthodox focus)	Heaven: children's ideas of heaven	Pages 11–12 See also *Developing Primary RE: Jesus* pages 27–28

Exploring Easter with younger pupils

For the teacher

The concept of 'resurrection' is particularly difficult – and not only for young children. However, this is the fundamental belief of the Christian faith, the key aspect of Easter, and the most important festival in the Christian calendar. For children aged 4–7, understanding of this concept is developed through exploring symbols associated with new life, celebrations and the re-telling of the Easter story.

Activity for pupils 1: New life

Copy the picture cards on page 7. They can either be cut up into individual cards or left as one sheet. Pupils can:

→ identify the pictures, match them up and say why they have matched one particular picture with another;
→ identify what the pictures have in common and how they are different;
→ say why the image at the bottom of the page matches the words;
→ listen to the Easter story.

Reinforce key words: Jesus, Easter, new life.

Activity for pupils 2: Special days and Sundays

You will need seven large cards with a day of the week on each one, placed around the room.

→ Discuss the meanings of 'special' and 'celebration'.
→ What is your special day in the week? Go to the place in the classroom that has your special day on it.
→ Talk to the others at your special day point about why it is special to you.
→ Listen to the story of a very special day (the story of the first Easter Sunday).
→ What day in the week do you think is special for Christians? What do they celebrate on this day?
→ Use the mind-mapping activity on page 4 to draw together learning and to provide evidence of children's achievement.

Fact File: Easter eggs

- In some **Christian traditions** (e.g. Greek Orthodox), boiled eggs are dyed or painted red, symbolising the blood of Christ.
- **Pysanka** is the art of decorating eggs in the Ukraine. The designs and colours are often symbolic, e.g. rings around the egg = life without end; red = love.
- **Games** with decorated boiled eggs at Easter include knocking an opponent's egg with your own – the winner is the one whose egg cracks last. (Some say this symbolises the rolling away of the stone in front of the tomb.)

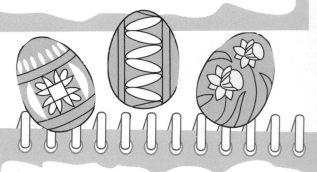

See also...

- *Tattybogle* by Sandra Horn and Ken Brown (1995, Hodder Children's Books, ISBN 0-340-65677-8): *a scarecrow is transformed into a beautiful tree – a lovely story for younger children paralleling the Easter message of new life.*
- *Rechenka's Eggs* by Patricia Polacco (Philomel Books, 1988): *Baboushka's beautiful painted eggs are broken by a goose, who gives something much greater in return – a story about new life.*
- *The Lion Storyteller Bible* (ISBN 0-7459-2921-4)
- *The Lion First Bible* (ISBN 0-7459-3210-X)

Can you match these pictures?

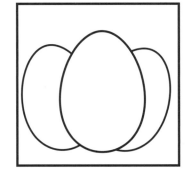

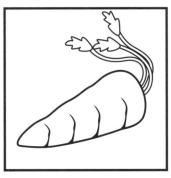

=

Jesus
Easter
new life

Activity for pupils 3: The Easter garden

For the teacher

→ Ask pupils to imagine they are with the women or in the garden watching everything happen.

→ Read the story, pausing often to allow the pupils to imagine the scene.

→ Ask pupils to talk about how they felt, and how the women might have felt.

→ Enlarge, copy and cut out the boxes in the grid below. Pupils could match facial expressions to words, and then sort and stick the boxes in the correct order. Finish by completing the sentence starter box and sticking it on to the page.

→ Pupils can demonstrate their understanding of how the women felt by describing or drawing an occasion when they had a shock or a surprise.

→ Use the face and sentence starter activity at the end to help pupils reflect on why they think Easter is a special time for Christians.

In the garden
Based on Matthew 28:1–10

It was very early in the morning and still quite dark, but some women friends of Jesus were already up. They were sad because only two days ago Jesus had died. Today, they were going to visit the place where he was buried. It was in a large and beautiful garden. The tomb had been cut out of solid rock and after Jesus' body had been laid there a huge stone was pushed in front of it. It was getting lighter now. They smelt the fresh dew on the grass, and felt it, wet against their legs. Suddenly, the earth started to shake, and shake. It was an earthquake! The women were frightened. But then something much more scary happened! Right before them an angel appeared and rolled the heavy stone away from the tomb. The women didn't know if they should stay or run away, but the angel spoke to them. What he said shocked them. He said: 'Don't be afraid, Jesus has been raised from the dead.' He showed them the place where Jesus had lain, and the white clothes that Jesus had been wrapped in just lay in a heap. He told the women to go and tell Jesus' other friends, the disciples, what had happened.

The women left the tomb quickly, still a bit scared but full of happiness and joy too. Then they had the best surprise of all. Can you guess what it was? Jesus himself was standing there, right in front of them. 'Do not be afraid,' he said.

Draw one of these faces in each box. The faces will show how the women in the story were feeling.

 = happy

= sad

 = worried

The women go to the garden early on the Sunday morning.	Suddenly there is an earthquake. An angel appears and rolls the stone away from the tomb.	The women run to tell the disciples what has happened.	They meet Jesus and he tells them not to be afraid.

Christians are on Easter Sunday because they believe

Easter activities for older pupils

Exploring humility and service to others through the story of Jesus washing his disciples' feet

For the teacher

- After the Last Supper, Jesus **washes his disciples' feet**. Usually **servants** did this. The story is told in John 13.
- For Christians this powerful story is about **humility** and **service** to others. It is retold on page 10 in a way designed to engage **7–9-year-old pupils**.
- The activities outlined below aim to help pupils to **explore and respond** to the themes of humility and service.

Telling the story...

- 'Guided story' is a powerful way of **drawing children into a story**. Use a stilling exercise* to establish a quiet and reflective atmosphere. Ask the children to **picture the scene** as you tell the story, imagining they are part of it. Leave plenty of pauses for them to **reflect** on their thoughts and feelings.
- This guided story can be **adapted** depending on the class, current media personalities and so on. It is a **modern retelling**, putting a person children can **relate** to in the place of Jesus. Ask pupils to picture someone they **respect**, perhaps a current sports hero.

After the guided story...

- Whose feet did the children choose to wash? Why?

Let pupils know that this story is like one the Bible tells about Jesus. It shows Jesus being humble and serving others. Read the story in a children's Bible (John 13).

The following activity allows each pupil to **do something nice** for others (service), and to have **something nice done for them** (humility in accepting and offering compliments).

Activity for pupils: Serving others

→ Give each pupil a piece of paper. They write their **name** at the **top** and pass it on to the person on their right.

→ Each pupil **reads the name** at the top of their new piece of paper and writes down something **nice** about that person at the **bottom,** e.g. a **skill** or **quality** they have, something others **admire**, something which makes them **unique**... **Fold** the paper up from the bottom to cover what has been written. Then the papers are passed on again.

→ **Repeat** until each child has their own piece of paper back. Give the children time to **read what others have said** about them and to **share** this with a friend.

→ With their partners, pupils **write a list** of **ten Random Acts of Kindness** which they **could do for others** if they have all the **gifts and qualities** on their paper.

→ These lists could form the basis of **role-plays**, which pupils could plan and act out in pairs: How will they use their **gifts** to **serve** others?

Things to note

These activities complement QCA scheme of work Unit 4C 'Why is Easter important to Christians?'

* Stilling exercise: for more information, see *A to Z: Practical Learning Strategies*, Mackley and Draycott (eds), RE Today Services, 2004, page 60.

Love is... *serving each other*

A guided story: Being humble and serving others

Imagine that, as we are all sitting here, we are awaiting a visit from a very important person: David Beckham is coming to our school. Imagine that it has been a hot day and you are all feeling sweaty after games. You'd love to get showered and changed but the head teacher is making you all stand in line in the heat, on your best behaviour. You are feeling excited — you think about David Beckham's great skill in scoring goals. He's so talented. You begin to wonder if he'll stop to talk to you or if he'll just walk straight past you without noticing you. Will he be friendly to you, or is he so great and famous that he won't even look your way? Will he just want to see the important people? Suddenly, you see a big Rolls Royce draw up outside and he steps out of the car. You hold your breath, straining to see — the excitement is unbearable! You can't believe it! David Beckham is actually walking into your classroom! Everyone is looking up at him. How will he act? Is he too famous to talk to any of you, or will he smile in your direction? Take a few moments to imagine what you think might happen next...

...pause...

Very quietly, you watch as David does something completely unexpected. He picks up a towel and walks over to the sink. 'You all look hot and tired after your game,' he says, looking at you all. You carry on watching as he fills a bowl of water and takes it over to someone in your class. Puzzled, you watch as he takes off their trainers and their socks — and washes their feet! Their smelly, sweaty feet!! 'I know how sweaty and uncomfortable I feel after a match,' he says. 'That should be better,' he adds as he dries their feet with the towel. You realise that the person he has chosen shoots the best goals in the whole class — perhaps David knows that and that's why he chose them. But then he goes over to someone who doesn't like playing football, someone who hardly knows who David Beckham is, and he washes his feet too and chats to him for a while. Now you are feeling really confused ... Why is he behaving like this? Why would someone so great be so humble?...

...pause...

You watch David going round the class, washing everyone's feet, and gradually you realise that he will come to you and wash your feet too. How does that make you feel...? What will you say to him?... Picture that scene and notice your feelings ... David washes your feet and as he dries them he says, 'Go and do the same,' and he hands you the bowl and the towel, and he leaves... Take a few moments to imagine what you do next... where do you take the bowl...? Whose feet will you wash...?

...pause...

Understanding Easter

For the teacher

For Christians, Easter is not just something which happened nearly 2,000 years ago, but something which has significance and power in the present. The activities outlined here will enable upper primary pupils to show that they can:

- **interpret** the meaning of Christian symbols;
- **identify** which parts of the Holy Week story the symbols represent;
- **sequence** correctly the events leading up to Easter Sunday;
- **evaluate** which symbols might have the deepest significance for Christians today, giving thoughtful reasons for their answers;
- **design**, using colour and shape:
  - their own symbol of the meaning of Easter for Christians;
  - a picture expressing their own ideas and questions about heaven.

Activity for upper primary pupils

This activity can be used: to establish prior learning at the start of a teaching unit; to link information learned one year with that learned in the next; or to assess the amount of learning that has occurred at the end of the topic.

Organise the class into pairs, and give each pair a set of the cards below. Ask them to:

→ **identify** each of the symbols and say which part of the Holy Week story it connects with;

→ **sequence** the symbols in the correct order to match the events of Holy Week, starting out with Palm Sunday through to Easter Day (There are two 'red herrings' – can pupils pick them out?);

→ **decide** together which part of the story is most important to Christians today and **explain why**;

→ **design** a lapel badge a Christian today would be proud to wear to show his or her beliefs.

Matthew 26:26–28	John 13:1–15	Mark 15:15–23	Mark 11:1–11
Luke 23:44–49	John 19:17	Luke 22:47–53	Matthew 2:1–2
Mark 16:1–8	Mark 14:32–42	Luke 22:4–6	Matthew 21:12–17
I don't know him Luke 22:54–62	Mark 15:1–5	Mark 10:13–16	Matthew 22:15–22

Resurrection and heaven

For the teacher

Easter in an Orthodox Christian community provides a rich and highly visual resource for exploring two related Christian ideas with pupils: resurrection and heaven.

The information below highlights some of the key points which teachers might find helpful when introducing the activities to pupils.

The meaning of Easter for Orthodox Christians

On Sunday morning the Resurrection of our Lord and God and Saviour Jesus Christ is our joy and our whole life as Orthodox Christians. Without Pascha (Easter) there is no Christianity, no gospel, no hope. In the joy of the resurrection all shall be brought to life!   *www.antiochian-orthodox.co.uk*

Expressing beliefs about heaven

An Orthodox church is more than a building in which to meet. Its very architecture and art speak volumes about the relationship that exists between God and man, for example:

The dome

The shape of the dome symbolises how, in Jesus, the things of earth and the things of heaven are brought together. The inside of the dome is often illustrated with the risen Christ reigning in heaven.

The nave

The nave (main body) of the church is usually rectangular, like a ship. This is the place for God's people, both those alive now and those who have lived in earlier times, and whose images are visible from the nave in icons and frescos.

Colour

Colour is used everywhere to illustrate key beliefs and themes. Symbolic colours include:

- light blue – Mary;
- gold – the Kingdom of God;
- purple or black – darkness;
- white – Jesus;
- blue – heaven;
- green – the Holy Spirit.

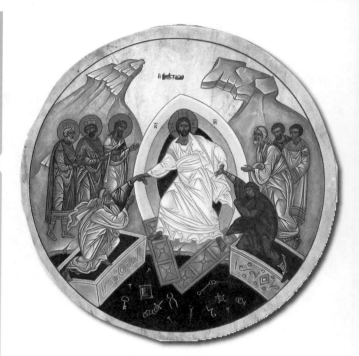

Resurrection
www.ateliersaintandre.net/en/ pages/latest_work/marble.html

Activities for upper primary pupils

→ **Show pupils** a traditional Orthodox picture of the resurrection, such as the one above (examples can easily be found on the internet and in books). Ask them to:

- **identify** the beliefs about resurrection the artist is giving and how they achieve this (e.g. colour, shape, position, gesture);
- **make links** between the picture and the biblical story (note the tools in the foreground);
- **suggest** how the people in the picture might be feeling, and why (prompt with the quotation on this page).

→ **Draw or show** pupils the shape of a dome. Ask them to:

- **make links** between the picture of resurrection and the shape;
- **suggest** why a dome might be a good shape to use in a church, and speculate about what might be painted inside it;
- **design** their own picture for the inside of a dome, expressing their own ideas and questions about heaven.

Divali: Lakshmi – goddess of good fortune

For the teacher

The following activities use a range of learning intelligences to explore the significance of Lakshmi and the festival of Divali for Hindus today. The activities encourage pupils to:

- explore and interpret a visual image of the Hindu goddess Lakshmi;
- use speaking and listening skills to ask and respond to probing questions;
- reflect on blessings, good fortune, kindness and generosity.

As a result of these activities, pupils should be able to:

- *identify some ways in which Hindus celebrate Divali and describe three ways in which some Hindus show devotion to Lakshmi;*
- *ask some questions and suggest some answers about the celebration and significance of Divali for Hindus.*
  (Level 4 – QCA expectations)

Fact file: Divali and Lakshmi

- **Divali** is the Hindu festival of lights marking the beginning of the new year.
- It normally occurs during **October**. It is celebrated in a variety of ways in different parts of India and in different Hindu communities. **Diva lamps** are often lit during this festival, and so it is often referred to as a festival of lights.
- Puja (prayer) to Lakshmi is common at Divali.
- **Lakshmi** is the shakti (consort or wife) of **Vishnu** and is born whenever he is born. When he descends as **Rama** she is born as **Sita**, when he is **Krishna** she is **Radha** and later **Rukmini**.
- She is the goddess of wealth, good fortune and beauty. Worshippers pray to her for health and prosperity for their family.

Things to note...

These activities complement QCA RE scheme of work Unit 3B: 'How and why do Hindus celebrate Divali?' – Section 4: 'How do Hindus see God?'

See also...

Websites for images of Lakshmi and other Hindu gods and goddesses:
www.hindunet.org
www.sanatansociety.org
www.strath.ac.uk/Departments/SocialStudies/RE/Database

Complexion golden yellow symbolising wealth bringer, or pink as the mother of all

Sari white for purity

Giver of protection and blessing

Gold coins fall from her 'gift-giving hand' – the bringer of prosperity and wealth

Stands on lotus – symbol of divine truth

Activity for pupils: Exploring an image of Lakshmi

→ Provide groups of pupils with an image of the goddess Lakshmi. These can be downloaded from a website and printed (if possible in colour) in the middle of an A3 sheet of paper. Alternatively, display on an interactive whiteboard for whole-class activity.

→ Ask pupils, in small groups, to look very carefully at the 'person'. Use the prompt questions to structure pupils' thinking. These can be displayed or given out on prompt cards.

→ Ask pupils to think about what the image tells them about the kind of 'person' they are looking at, and at least two questions they would like to ask the 'person' if they had the chance. (Younger pupils or pupils who find writing difficult can contribute to discussion with someone else scribing their responses.)

→ Follow up by gathering pupils' responses and recording around a whiteboard image of Lakshmi, noting how many groups said similar things. Draw conclusions about what has been learned about Lakshmi from looking at her image.

→ Explore the questions pupils would like to ask Lakshmi. Get the pupils to suggest how they think she might answer. If possible, ask a Hindu parent or friend of the school to take part in this activity.

→ Draw the discussion together by introducing the concept of symbolism, reinforcing how the image of Lakshmi is symbolic for Hindus. Talk about Lakshmi, and about how she is worshipped at Divali time by many Hindus as the goddess of good fortune, wealth and new beginnings.

Questions for pupils

What does this picture tell you about Lakshmi?

What do her clothes and other things she is wearing tell you about her?

Why do you think she has four arms?

What are her hands doing and why?

Look at the expression on her face – what sort of person do you think she is?

What questions would you ask her if you could?

For the teacher

Follow-up class discussion: your questions will depend on pupils' responses, for example:

Four groups said she looks kind – what made you think that?

Six groups said she was rich or wealthy – what evidence do you have to back that up?

Three groups said she was generous – why do you think this?

Questions they would like to ask: focus on why they want to ask the question and how she might answer.

Below are some examples of children's responses when doing this activity.

What does she look like and how does she make you feel?

She is very pretty and rich.

She is not wearing shoes.

She has four arms.

She looks peaceful.

She looks happy.

She is jenrus. *(sic – generous)*

She has a calm feeling.

Her eyes made us feel peaceful.

She made us feel happy because she is happy.

What would you like to ask her?

Why do you have four arms?

Why are you holding that flower?

You look happy. Are you?

Who gave you all your jewellery?

Why are you dropping stones on the ground? *(needed to be corrected – not stones, but coins)*

Blessings and good fortune for the world
A discussion and display activity for upper primary pupils

For the teacher

• Hindus believe that Brahman, the universal spirit, is beyond human understanding but that each god and goddess gives a clue as to what God is like. **Lakshmi** shows the divine as **generous, kind and loving**, the **bringer of good fortune** to those who worship her.

This activity aims to enable pupils to apply the idea of **Lakshmi** as the **bringer of blessings and good fortune** to their own experience of the world.

Expectations

By the end of this activity, pupils should be able to:

• understand that many Hindus pray to **Lakshmi** for 'good fortune' at **Divali** time;

• express their own ideas about what such '**blessings**' and '**good fortune**' for the world might actually be;

• suggest ways in which each one of us could help to bring such a world about.

→ Give each pupil a large copy of the framework below. Explain that they are to think about the '**good fortune**' that **Hindus** ask **Lakshmi** to bring at Divali. What might this be for their school and the world around them?

→ Individually pupils reflect on, and write in, the 'blessings' and 'good fortune' they think would improve their own lives, those of their friends or family members, and the school and the world generally.

→ Get together in groups to share ideas. Focus on school (3), community (4) and world (5). Decide together on one suggestion in each category to focus on.

→ On circles of gold card (coin shapes) each pupil produces a drawing and writing about the topic agreed by the group – on one side a picture, on the other what they think should be done to make things better in this respect. The completed work is then put together so that each group's 'coins' for 3, 4 and 5 are strung together respectively. Display these in the classroom, hanging them from the ceiling like coins falling from Lakshmi's hand.

→ Individually, pupils can choose either 1 or 2 and write a few sentences about what 'blessings' or 'good fortune' they hope to bring about for themselves or their friends and family, and how they might do this.

Lakshmi

Bringer of blessings and good fortune

1 For myself
2 For a friend or family member
3 For the school
4 For the local community
5 In the world generally

Celebrating Divali

For the teacher

As part of **Divali** celebrations, Hindus light **diva lamps** to encourage **Lakshmi** to come to them to bring the blessing of **good fortune** for the coming year.

This custom is symbolic of the way in which, for Hindus, the divine is welcomed into everyday life.

Here is a brief explanation of how **Ashish** and **Prakash** (two brothers living in London) and their family celebrate **Divali**.

See also...

The most significant story told at Divali is the story of Rama and his wife Sita.

See **Developing Primary RE: Faith Stories** (RE Today Services, 2003) pages 18–21 for activities for exploring this story with pupils.

Ashish and Prakash celebrate Divali

Divali is a very special time for us. Our mum spends a lot of time cleaning the house in preparation for the festival – she makes us help too! She and our aunty and grandma do lots of cooking. They make lots of sweets. We also go shopping for new clothes to wear. The house is decorated with red swastikas. The Hindu one is different from the Nazi one!! Ours is an ancient symbol of good luck. There are also lots of candles and divas (oil lamps) about the house so that it is full of light. We also put divas on the steps to our house and down the path – this is to welcome Lakshmi, the goddess of light into our house for the celebrations and to ask her to bring us good luck for the coming year. Our family join together and sometimes friends come too – as it starts to get dark we offer puja (worship) to Lakshmi and then we have a nice meal of different curries and rice and breads, but we leave room for the sweets mum has made for us! After this we have fireworks in the garden. We believe Lakshmi is very important because she brings good luck. She is kind and generous and wants us to be kind and generous too.

An activity for younger pupils

→ Talk about when a special visitor comes to your house. How do you prepare for the visit? Why is such care taken?

→ Read to the pupils about how **Ashish** and **Prakash** prepare for Divali, for welcoming Lakshmi into their home.

→ Prepare the home corner for Divali. Tidy and clean it, add flowers and lots of 'lit candles' made from sweets tubes covered in white paper with a 'flame' of yellow or orange tissue. Place a statue or picture of Lakshmi in it. Sit in the home corner and talk about ways of being kind and generous to one another. Share some sweets before going home.

Activities for upper primary pupils

In pairs: read together about how Ashish and Prakash prepare for Divali. Make a list of the key points of what they do to prepare, and on the day itself. Compare these practices with those from a different religion's festival (e.g. Christmas in Christianity or Hanukkah in Judaism). What are the similarities and what are the differences?

On your own: Hindus believe Lakshmi is generous and kind. Think of an occasion when someone has shown generosity to you. How did it make you feel? Express your feelings in the form of a poem using either an acrostic or haiku form. Display the poems in the classroom.

Id-ul-Fitr and Id-ul-Adha: special times in Islam

Fact file: Id-ul-Fitr

- Ramadan, the Muslim month of fasting, ends with a celebration called **Id-ul-Fitr**. This is one of the two main festivals of Islam. The other is Id-ul-Adha.

- Id means 'recurring happiness' It is a feast for thanking Allah and celebrating a happy occasion. It is a joyful day, a religious holiday. Gifts and cards are exchanged. Children wear new clothes.

- **Id-ul-Fitr** marks the end of Ramadan, when Muslims have learned self-discipline, a sense of harmony and community, and during which they remember their duty to the poor.

- Before prayers at Id, a charity donation is paid: Zakat-ul-Fitr.

- At Id, Muslims attend prayers at the mosque.

- The emphasis on community continues as neighbours visit each other and exchange greetings.

Activity for lower primary pupils: Celebrating and remembering

Id-ul-Fitr is an annual joyful **celebration**.

- Brainstorm some special celebrations pupils have taken part in. Talk about how a particular special occasion, such as a birthday, was celebrated: for example, clothes they might wear; who helped them to celebrate; how they celebrated.

- Muslims exchange **gifts and cards** at Id like at a birthday. If pupils were to write a card to themselves to commemorate the most important things they have done and learned since their last birthday, what would they include? Use a framework like the one below to structure and sort children's ideas. Gather pupils' writing and drawings together inside a large folded card.

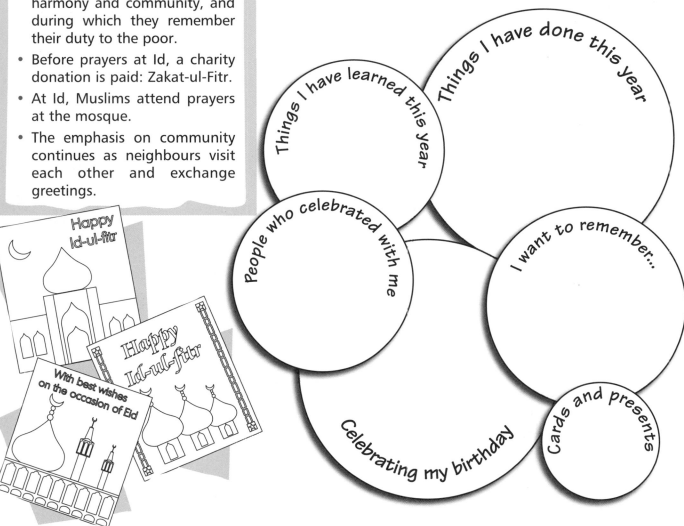

Activity for upper primary pupils: Exploring the meaning of Id-ul-Fitr

The main features of Id-ul-Fitr are:
- giving to charity;
- prayers at the mosque;
- clothes and cards;
- remembering the lessons of Ramadan;
- visits to neighbours.

The following activity will help pupils to explore these features and to develop an understanding of the meaning of Id-ul-Fitr for Muslims:

➜ Pupils research, using ICT and textbooks, what Muslims do and remember at Id. Try to provide resources which describe Id from the point of view of individual young Muslims. The best resource would be a Muslim visitor who can talk to the children and answer questions.

➜ Encourage reflection on parallels with pupils' own experiences by using sentence starters such as:
- A time I did something for charity was...
- A 'community' I belong to is... Together we...
- I wore special clothes and celebrated by giving and receiving gifts when...
- An event which made me feel close to other people was...

➜ Give each pupil an enlarged copy of the Islamic star shape. Pupils fill in factual information about Id on the front of the star and why these are important for Muslims. On the back, they could write about one of their own parallel experiences. Decorate with Islamic designs and display as mobiles.

With best wishes
on the occasion of Eid
We pray
Allah Subhana Wa ta Ala
to bless you
and the Islamic Ummah
with His unbounded grace

See also...

Books for teachers
Teaching RE 5–11: Islam (RE Today Services)
Islam: A Pictorial Guide (RE Today Services)

Videos
Pathways of Belief: Islam (BBC)
Speaking for Ourselves (RMEP)

Websites
http://re-xs.ucsm.ac.uk
www.holidays.net/ramadan
www.bbc.co.uk/religion/religions/islam
www.atschool.eduweb.co.uk/carolrb/islam/festivals.html

For the teacher: Expectations

It is important to be clear about what you want pupils to know, understand and be able to do by the end of the teaching activity. Below you will see two 'I can' statements which describe such outcomes in a pupil-friendly way. These are based on the QCA expectations for most pupils aged 11, matched to the content of the above teaching suggestions.

I *can* make links between Id, Ramadan and my own experiences of celebrating and self-denial...

I *can* ask some questions and suggest some answers about those things which matter most to a Muslim (e.g. values such as belonging to a community, worshipping Allah, caring for those in need).

For you to do...

Use books and ICT to find out how Muslims celebrate the festival of Id-ul-Fitr.

Use these headings to help you:

- Giving to charity
- Prayers at the mosque
- Clothes and cards
- Remembering the lessons of Ramadan
- Visits to neighbours

Display your findings, using words and pictures, on a star shape as below.

Giving to charity

Visits to neighbours

Prayers at the mosque

What does Id-ul-Fitr mean for Muslims?

Remembering Ramadan

Clothes and cards

My experience of...

On the back of the star, write and draw about your own experience using one or more of the sentence starters your teacher will give you.

Decorate your star using shapes and symbols that would be pleasing for a Muslim.

Id-ul-Adha – festival of sacrifice

Fact file: Id-ul-Adha

- This is the other big festival celebrated by Muslims every year. It coincides with the completion of Hajj (pilgrimage to Makkah).

- It commemorates the time when Ibrahim was going to sacrifice his son to prove obedience to God. Muslims consider that Ibrahim (Abraham) was a prophet or messenger from God.

- Muslims go to the mosque together for prayers. Later in the day they sacrifice a sheep, and give one third of the meat away to friends and a third to the poor.

- The festival is also known as Id-ul-Kabir (the Greater Id) or, in Turkish, Qurban Bayram (feast of sacrifice).

The story of Ibrahim and Isma'il

The prophet Ibrahim (Abraham) was asked by Allah to make many sacrifices. One was to leave his home, all that he knew and was familiar with, to travel with his family to Makkah. Despite his fears he was obedient to Allah and went. When they arrived Allah ordered him to build the house of Allah (the Ka'bah). He and his son Isma'il (Ishmael) worked very hard building the house. Whilst they were working on the Ka'bah, the Angel Jibril (Gabriel) was sent by Allah with a message. A stone from heaven called Har-ul-Aswad was to be added to one of its walls. Again Ibrahim obeyed – it is this black stone that to this present day is visible in the Ka'bah and which pilgrims try to touch as they circle the great building.

After they had finished building the Ka'bah Allah appeared to Ibrahim in a dream and told him to set off to Mina where he was to sacrifice his precious son, Isma'il. Along the way the devil (Shaytan/Iblis) tried to tempt Ibrahim but he stayed true to Allah's wishes and drove the devil away. As Ibrahim was about to sacrifice his son Allah stopped him and gave him a sheep to sacrifice instead. The complete obedience of Ibrahim is celebrated every year at Id-ul-Adha when Muslims remember the necessity of their own submission to the will of Allah and their need to be willing to sacrifice anything that Allah wishes.

The Qur'an (Surah 37:102.12)

Things to note...

- This story is also found in the Jewish scriptures or Christian Old Testament (Genesis 22), with one important difference. In the Judeo-Christian story God asks Abraham to sacrifice his other son Isaac, his son with Sarah. Isma'il is his son with Hagar. See also *Developing Primary RE: Faith Stories* (RE Today Services), pages 24–25.

- The activities in this unit complement QCA non-statutory scheme of work Unit 5B: How do Muslims express their religious beliefs through practice?

Overcoming temptation

Stoning the Devil

The **Hajj** is a **pilgrimage** that takes place every year, when **Muslims** from all over the world travel to **Makkah**, in Saudi Arabia, to take part. Something that happens during the **Hajj** is the '**stoning of the Devil**'. The **pilgrims** throw pebbles at a pillar known as the 'Great Devil'.

Why do you think they do this?

There are two reasons:

Firstly it reminds them of the story of how **Ibrahim** was **tempted** to sacrifice his son **Isma'il,** who in turn was tempted to run away. Neither of them gave in to **temptation** and they drove **the Devil** (**Shaytan** or **Iblis**) away by throwing stones at him.

What do you think made Ibrahim and Isma'il 'stone the Devil'?

Secondly, by 'stoning the Devil' they are showing their own **rejection of wrongdoing and evil** and showing their **commitment** to withstand the temptations that may come their way just as **Ibrahim** and **Isma'il** did all those years ago.

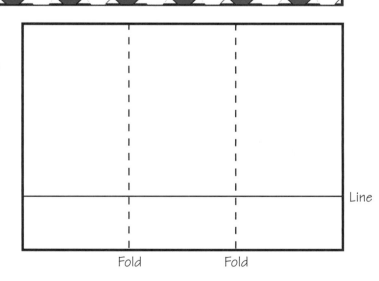

How might 'stoning the Devil' as part of Hajj help a Muslim to live a better life?

Personal reflection

Turn a plain piece of A4 paper landscape-way, and fold it into thirds.

Draw a line 5cm from the bottom across the page.

In each section, write or draw an occasion when you were tempted to do wrong.

Think about whether or not you 'gave in' or 'resisted' the temptation, and why.

Under each 'temptation', write two or three sentences explaining your thoughts about this.

Fold   Fold

Line

(This piece of paper is for your eyes only – you need not share any of it with others in the class or even with your teacher if you don't want to.)

Making a sacrifice

Id-ul-Adha

- Id-ul-Adha is known as the 'festival of sacrifice' because whilst **pilgrims** on **Hajj** are sacrificing their animals near to **Makkah**, they are joined by **Muslims** across the world in making an animal sacrifice (of a sheep or goat).

- One third is eaten by the **family**, one third is given to **friends and relatives**; and one third is given to the **poor**. Some Muslims who live in the United Kingdom might choose to send money to Pakistan or India, for example, to pay for an animal to be sacrificed there and its meat given to feed the poor.

Why do Muslims make a sacrifice at Eid?

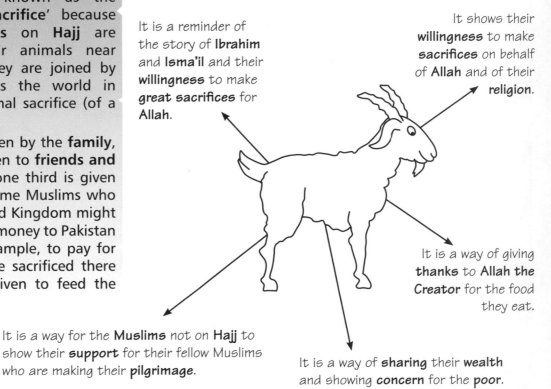

It is a reminder of the story of **Ibrahim** and **Isma'il** and their **willingness** to make **great sacrifices** for Allah.

It shows their **willingness** to make **sacrifices** on behalf of Allah and of their **religion**.

It is a way for the **Muslims** not on **Hajj** to show their **support** for their fellow Muslims who are making their **pilgrimage**.

It is a way of giving **thanks** to Allah **the Creator** for the food they eat.

It is a way of **sharing** their **wealth** and showing **concern** for the **poor**.

In small groups

Brainstorm the word '**sacrifice**' and talk about the different aspects of its meaning.

Think of five **different kinds** of 'sacrifice' people might have to make (e.g. giving up chocolate to lose weight, going without any food so that you can feed your child, etc.). Join with another group and share your ideas.

Through group discussion agree to put the different 'sacrifices' you have thought of into **order**. Put the most 'sacrificial' at the top and work down your list. Be prepared to share your ideas and the order with the rest of the class – so **reasons** are important.

On your own

Ibrahim was tested to **sacrifice** his own child, someone very **close** and **important** to him.

Write an **acrostic poem** reflecting your understanding of the word '**sacrifice**'.

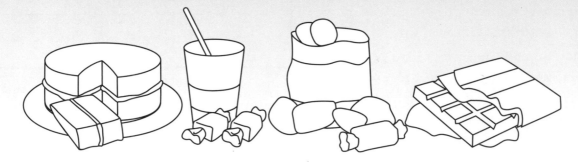

Pesach – a festival of freedom and hope

Fact file: Pesach (Passover)

- Pesach is celebrated in memory of the Exodus, the escape from slavery in Egypt at the time of Moses. It is a festival of freedom and hope, reminding Jews of how G-d acted to keep the promise (covenant) he had made with them.

- It takes place in the springtime and is one of the three ancient pilgrim festivals of Judaism, the others being **Shavuot** (summer), marking the giving of the Ten Commandments, and **Sukkot** (autumn), which commemorates the journey through the desert on the way to the Promised Land.

- Pesach celebrations are highly symbolic:
  - During the festival all yeast or leaven (chametz) is forbidden. It reminds Jews of the haste with which their ancestors left Egypt (having no time to wait for their bread to rise) and is a symbol of pride since leaven 'puffs things up'. **Matzot** (unleavened bread) can be purchased at many supermarkets.
  - The main event is the Seder meal – a ceremonial meal at which the story of the original Passover is told from the Hagadah.
  - The Seder plate with its symbolic foods is a visual way of retelling these events. Page 28 outlines a reflective activity for children using the symbolism of this plate.

- The Promised Land is the goal towards which the freed Israelites set out. This land, the modern state of Israel, is the embodiment for Jewish people of the **covenant** or promise made between them and God. The Pesach Seder meal finishes with the proclamation 'Next year in Jerusalem. Next year may all be free!' The ongoing tensions in the Middle East reflect different attitudes towards 'ownership' of this land. Pupils may well be aware of these from the news and teachers need to exercise sensitivity in responding to pupils' questions and issues.

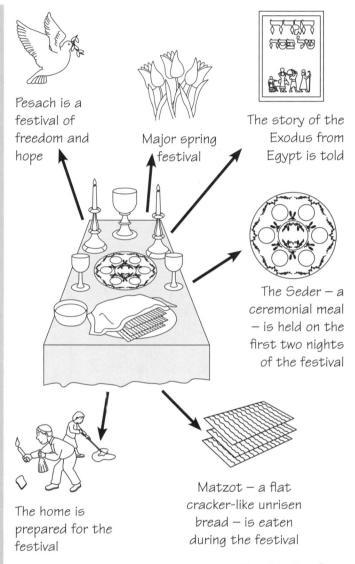

Pesach is a festival of freedom and hope

Major spring festival

The story of the Exodus from Egypt is told

The Seder – a ceremonial meal – is held on the first two nights of the festival

The home is prepared for the festival

Matzot – a flat cracker-like unrisen bread – is eaten during the festival

See also...

RE Today Services books for teachers
Teaching RE 5–11: Judaism
Judaism: A Pictorial Guide

Some useful websites
www.jewfaq.org/holidaya.htm – includes audio files of music for the songs sung during the Seder
www.torahtots.com/holidays/pesach/pesach.htm – detailed and interactive for children
www.holidays.net/passover – information and music files

Exploring Pesach – creative and expressive activities for lower primary pupils

The following activities explore the feelings associated with Pesach.
Key theme: the joy of freedom.
Teaching strategy: creative and expressive activities using colours, art, mime, music and dance.

Activity for pupils 1: Feelings of slavery and freedom

Re-tell the story of the Israelites being freed from slavery and beginning their journey to the Promised Land.

Paired talk: What do you think it felt like to be a slave? How do you think they felt when they were set free?

Class activity: share ideas listing adjectives on a 'feelings board' under two headings: 'slaves' and 'free'.

Use colours to express feelings: Ask children: If 'happy' could be a colour, what would it be? If 'frightened' was a colour, what would it be? Agree a colour to go by each of the feelings on the 'feelings board'. (If using an electronic whiteboard, use the colour palette to change the colour of each emotion as agreed).

Explain that Pesach is a very happy time for Jewish people today as they are remembering when their ancestors were set free. Agree three colours to represent Pesach. Ask children to design a poster to show how Jews feel about Pesach using these colours.

Activity for pupils 2: Using music to express freedom

Listen to four or five contrasting instrumental pieces of music (dark, slow, mournful/light, quick, vibrant). Ask children to think about how each makes them feel. Talk together about this.

Using the feelings board from activity one, ask pupils to say on which side they would place each piece of music.

Vote to decide which piece of music best represents the happy feelings associated with being freed from slavery. Play this piece of music again, getting the pupils to join in either using percussion instruments or clapping along to the rhythm.

Activity for pupils 3: Expressing freedom

This activity needs plenty of space for children to move about, so try to use the hall if possible.

→ Talk about how our bodily movements tell others how we are feeling without us ever having to say a word. Mime telling someone off, and ask the class to guess how you are feeling.

→ Divide the class into two. Give one half cards saying 'very sad'. Ask them to mime this feeling. Ask the observers to watch carefully, to think about how the others are feeling, and to think about how they know this (e.g. facial expressions, heads bowed, slow movement). Repeat the activity, this time with the other half miming being 'joyful'.

→ Remind children of the story of Pesach – the escape from slavery. In small groups of three or four, ask children to work out a dance or movement to show how the Israelites felt at the first Pesach. Give them strips of coloured cloth or ribbon (in the colours chosen in activity one) to tie around their wrists to accentuate movement. Set the movement to the joyful music chosen in activity two. Children could perform for each other and talk about how the Israelites must have felt and why.

Getting ready for Pesach

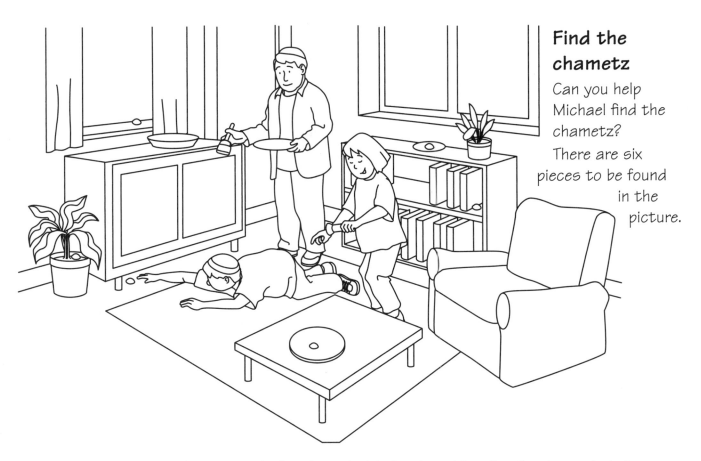

Find the chametz

Can you help Michael find the chametz?

There are six pieces to be found in the picture.

Michael is Jewish. To get ready for Pesach, Michael and his family clean their home and make sure that all chametz is gone. Chametz is anything made from grain with yeast in it to make it rise. Doing this helps them remember the time God helped their ancestors escape from slavery.

Colour in the picture of the bread that Daniel can eat during Pesach.

Getting your house ready for a special occasion – what could you do to help?

Exploring Pesach: Activities for lower primary pupils

Searching for chametz

Many religious celebrations begin with preparation of the home. Getting ready for Pesach involves spring cleaning to get rid of all prohibited (chametz) foods.

→ **Hear about and act out.** On the night before Pesach a symbolic search is made for breadcrumbs or foods containing yeast. Traditionally, ten pieces are hidden and the family searches with a candle (for light) and a feather (for sweeping). Use the stimulus sheet on page 25 to provide a starting point for exploring the practices and symbolism of Pesach with children.

Tasting Pesach foods

Watch a video or read about how the Seder meal is celebrated today. **Taste and explore the meaning** of some of the special foods, e.g. matzot (available from supermarkets), charoset (see recipe), salt water.

- **Matzot:** haste to leave Egypt – no time for the bread to rise.
- **Charoset:** reminds Jews of the mortar used by the slaves to build Pharaoh's cities, but the sweetness also reminds them of freedom.
- **Salt water:** symbol of the tears shed by the slaves in Egypt.

NB This is not a re-enactment or a simulation of a Seder meal.

Charoset

8 tablespoons of chopped nuts (walnuts, hazelnuts, almonds)

2 small cooking apples (peeled and grated)

2 teaspoons of cinnamon

A little strong red fruit juice (to bind)

Mix the ingredients together and bind with fruit juice.

Spoon into small pieces, enough for everyone, or spread on matzot and share around the class (being careful to warn children that this contains nuts).

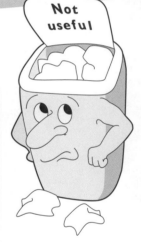

Thinking skills activities for upper primary pupils: Why do Michael and his family celebrate Pesach?

A mystery

→ In groups of three or four, pose pupils the above question. Set them the task of working together to 'solve' the mystery using the 'clues' provided on the information cards, some of which are 'red herrings' (page 27). Pupils will sort, group and evaluate the information to reach a conclusion to present to the class.

→ Each group presents their 'solution', giving reasons and justifications.

Useful for: getting pupils talking about their learning; developing thinking skills; a summative assessment activity.

A sorting and ranking activity

This provides a more structured variation of the above.

→ Working in groups, pupils are asked to pick out which nine statements are most informative to help them answer the question.

→ Provide each group with a target board and a dustbin shape. In turn, each person takes a card, reads it out and suggests where it should be placed. Other group members give their views and only when agreement is reached can the card be placed on the board or in the bin.

→ Each group presents their 'solution', giving reasons and justifications.

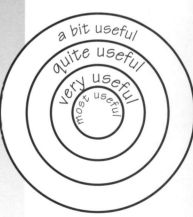

Why do Michael and his family celebrate Pesach?

They are Jewish	Michael's grandparents come to stay	It remembers God freeing the Israelites from slavery in Egypt
They spring-clean the house and get rid of all the chametz (yeast)	Chametz represents pride – not eating it shows they rely on God	It is when they use the special Pesach crockery and cutlery
Michael enjoys all the festivities	As the youngest person at the Seder meal he gets to ask the important questions	The Seder plate is very symbolic
The Seder plate helps to retell the story of what happened	The Seder plate is a reminder of the people's feelings	Michael likes to play football and to play games on the family computer
Michael goes to the synagogue with his dad and grandad	Celebrating Pesach makes Michael feel special	Michael's mum and dad take time off work
It is something that his family have always done	Celebrating Pesach helps him feel more Jewish	God told the people to celebrate the festival
It is a very happy family time	Eating the Seder meal together with family and friends is very important	Elijah's cup on the table reminds them that God is still at work in the world – the Messiah will come
It is the Feast of Unleavened Bread	It reminds them of God and of the Promised Land – next year in Jerusalem, next year may all be free!	The order for the celebration is written in the Haggadah

Photocopy onto thin card (laminate for extended use).
Cut into packs of cards and place in envelopes – one per group.
Reduce the number of statements as appropriate for some groups.

Learning from Pesach – using the Seder plate as a stimulus for reflection

Fact file

The Jewish festival of **Pesach** (Passover) is an annual remembrance and celebration of the key event in Jewish history when Moses led the people of Israel from slavery in Egypt to begin their long journey to freedom in the promised land.

As with many Jewish festivals, the home plays an important part in the festivities, and the **Seder meal** lies at the heart of the ceremonial.

During this meal, **symbolic foods** are eaten to remind the people of various aspects of their history and of their relationship with God – the **Seder plate** is used as a centre for this remembrance.

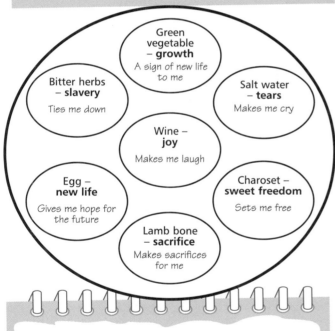

See also...

* **Developing Primary RE: Home and Family** (RE Today Services, 2003) – explores other Jewish artefacts and their significance.
* Video: **Animated World Faiths** (7–12) **Quest** series: **Moses and the Passover Meal** (www.4learningshop.co.uk)
* Links to QCA non-statutory Schemes of Work: Units 1E, 2C and 6A.

For the teacher

This 'learning from' activity encourages pupils to interpret the symbolic meaning of the items of food on the seder plate and relate them to their own experiences.

The activity can be matched to different ages or abilities by the number and type of Seder plate items selected for reflection. For example, Year 2 pupils could reflect on, and talk about, 'what makes me happy' and 'what makes me cry', whereas Year 4 might be encouraged to consider 'what ties me down'.

An activity for pupils

→ After watching or listening to the story of Pesach, explore with pupils how each item on the Seder plate represents or symbolises an important part of the event for Jewish people today.

→ In pairs, give pupils one item from the plate to look at and talk about. Ask them: *What is it? What part of the story does it represent? What does it tell you about how the Jewish people felt at the time?*

The diagram opposite identifies the feelings and experiences behind each item. Use this to help pupils reflect on their own experiences of crying, laughing, etc.

→ Give each pupil a paper plate (one for each aspect they are going to consider).

→ On one side, pupils draw something which makes them happy, hopeful, sad etc. On the reverse, they complete a sentence starter: '_____makes me happy/hopeful/sad because...', or whatever is applicable.

Pupils could talk about their drawing and writing with a partner. The completed plates could be displayed as mobiles.

(This idea is adapted from QCA's non-statutory guidance for Religious Education (2000) – **www.qca.org.uk**.)

Baisakhi – understanding Sikhs through festival

For the teacher

The activities suggested here use a visual approach, supported by probing questions. They aim to enable pupils to understand the meaning of the Sikh celebration of Baisakhi, and encourage reflection on their own celebrations in the light of this.

- Davinder's story, on page 30, is a fictionalised first-person account of the Baisakhi story.
- The copiable frames provide a visual framework and stimuli to help develop pupils' understanding of the story. This works well on an interactive whiteboard. The approach is a flexible strategy which can be applied to any 'people picture'. Visual starting points can lead to good thinking – avoid just asking pupils to 'draw a picture'!

Fact file: Sikh festivals

- Gurpurbs are Sikh festivals, or specials days. The word means 'Guru's day'.
- Baisakhi (also spelt 'Vaisakhi') is a worldwide Sikh celebration marking the founding of the Sikh Khalsa – the 'community of the pure' – in 1699.
- Community, commitment and self-sacrifice are the values central to this festival.
- The ritual of taking Amrit, which can be done at any time of life when they feel ready to make a 'commitment', has several purposes: a reminder of the founding of the Khalsa; a commitment to the Sikh faith; acceptance of a new adult member; and a visible sign of an inward faith expressed outwardly in the wearing of the Five Ks.
- Not all Sikhs are 'Amritdhari Sikhs', wearing the Five Ks and taking Amrit. This is a high aspiration of commitment.

Learning from Baisakhi: Probing questions to deepen learning

After exploring the story on page 30, ask pupils:

- When and why do people 'give something up'?
- Is 'giving something up' a sign of commitment? Is it always a good thing?
- 'To die for...' Can children think of other stories where people are prepared to die for something they believe in?
- Was the Guru fair on his followers, or is it too much to ask?
- What do pupils do to show their commitments, to family, pets, God, football? Does commitment always lead to action?
- Is the commitment to God different to other kinds of commitment?

Assessment
Using the activities and tasks as a way of gathering evidence of achievement

The frames for thinking about Sikh story, festival and ritual can be the basis of good assessment in RE. Teachers may like to share these 'I can...' statement with learners:

	Learning about the Sikh festival: I can...	Learning from Sikh commitments: I can...
Level 2	retell the story of Baisakhi.	ask a sensitive question about the Baisakhi story.
Level 3	link up the story to ways Sikhs celebrate today. suggest meanings for what happens in the story.	make links between what I celebrate and what Sikhs celebrate. talk about attitudes to 'giving things up'.
Level 4	show that I understand what Baisakhi, Amrit and the Five Ks have to do with commitment.	use my understanding of Sikh commitment to reflect on my own commitments.
Level 5	explain how and why Sikhs celebrate Baisakhi, take Amrit, wear the Five Ks. make connections between the festival, the story and the ritual.	explain clearly my own responses to the commitments of Guru Gobind Singh and the Sikhs, and explain my own commitments in the light of this.

Davinder's story

Let me introduce myself. I'm a 14-year-old girl and my name is Davinder Kaur – well, it is now! Let me tell you how it got changed!

Last month it was a special festival for us Sikhs. Our guru, who's called Guru Gobind Rai, sent a message round to us all to make a big effort to go to Anandpur for the festival. Our family had to walk for two days to get there. But I'm glad we went. You should have seen it: there were huge crowds, and people all up the hill, with a tent at the top. Our guru is a wonderful speaker. He gave a speech that day to change all our lives. We stood quite far back, but I had a good view. He was reminding us about being committed to the Sikh path, and ended up asking who would give something up for the faith. People offered money, time, and all sorts of different gifts – animals, or even a house (Sikhs are supposed to be generous). Then the guru lifted his head and spoke again: 'But who among you will give your life, your head, to show your commitment?' He brandished a sword. His eyes gleamed. The crowd fell silent, shocked ... for what seemed like ages. The breeze fluttered the tent. Then, quietly, a man stepped forward. 'I'm prepared to die for my faith,' he said, softly. The guru led him into the tent. The crowd stayed silent. There was a sickening sound from inside, a sort of thud. Then the guru came out again, with blood on his sword and his clothes. He called for another person willing to die for the faith. I tugged at dad's jacket and whispered, 'He didn't kill him, did he, Dad?' My dad motioned to me to be silent. I couldn't believe what I was seeing, it just felt horrible. But a second person did step forward. Into the tent he went. We heard the thudding chop of a sword, blood splashed onto the tent from inside. The guru did this five times altogether, with the crowd growing more and more uncomfortable. He seemed to be inside for ages.

Then the flap opened, and the guru walked out. Behind him came the five men. Suddenly the horrified silence broke. Everyone was gasping and crying, going crazy. At last, the guru got us all to listen again, and praised the five. We were all wondering what had happened inside, and what he had said – had he just been beheading some animals, goats or something? Had the five men been killed, and been brought back to life by a miracle?

We didn't get answers, but we did get a challenge. Guru Gobind Rai told us that he wanted more commitment from all of us. He named the five men as 'Panj Piares' (it means The Beloved Five), and asked us all to join him in becoming 'Khalsa'. He prepared a bowl of water, in which his wife Mata Sundri sprinkled sugar crystals. He sprinkled this Amrit from the iron bowl onto the eyes and heads of the five brave people, and each one showed their commitment. Again we gasped as the guru himself bowed down before these Five. We shouldn't have been surprised I suppose – he is a humble guru. He then gave them five symbols to wear, and new names. He said Sikh men should add 'Lion' (Singh) to their names, and Sikh women should add 'Princess' (Kaur) to theirs.

I can't really explain how we were feeling on the way home. Dad seemed very quiet. My sister was quite tearful. But we've all decided we are all going to be much more committed than we have been before. It was a great day, very emotional.

And now my guru is called Guru Gobind Singh, and my name is Davinder Kaur.

Explanation C

Festivals always re-tell old stories. Why does the story of the start of the Khalsa matter to Sikhs?

What puzzles me about the festival is...

Explanation D

Festivals can make people feel determined to be good. What does Baisakhi make people want to do?

I am feeling...

This is a great day because...

Look carefully at the picture of Baisakhi celebrations. Sikhs carry the Guru Granth Sahib around the outside of the Gurdwara. The 'Panj Piare' stand to attention. Other members of the community play music, look on, join in. What do they think and feel?

Think about the Baisakhi story and the celebrations with a partner. Fill in the thought bubbles above with the things you think Sikhs think about at the festival. Then fill in the explanation sections as well. Make it detailed and clear!

Explanation B

Festivals are always reminders. What does Baisakhi remind Sikhs about?

I will never forget...

Explanation A

Why do the Sikhs dress in this special way?

Explanation B
What do young Sikhs remember as they take Amrit?

Explanation A
What's happening in the picture?

I'm so proud of him today because…

This reminds me of the time when…

My feelings at this moment are…

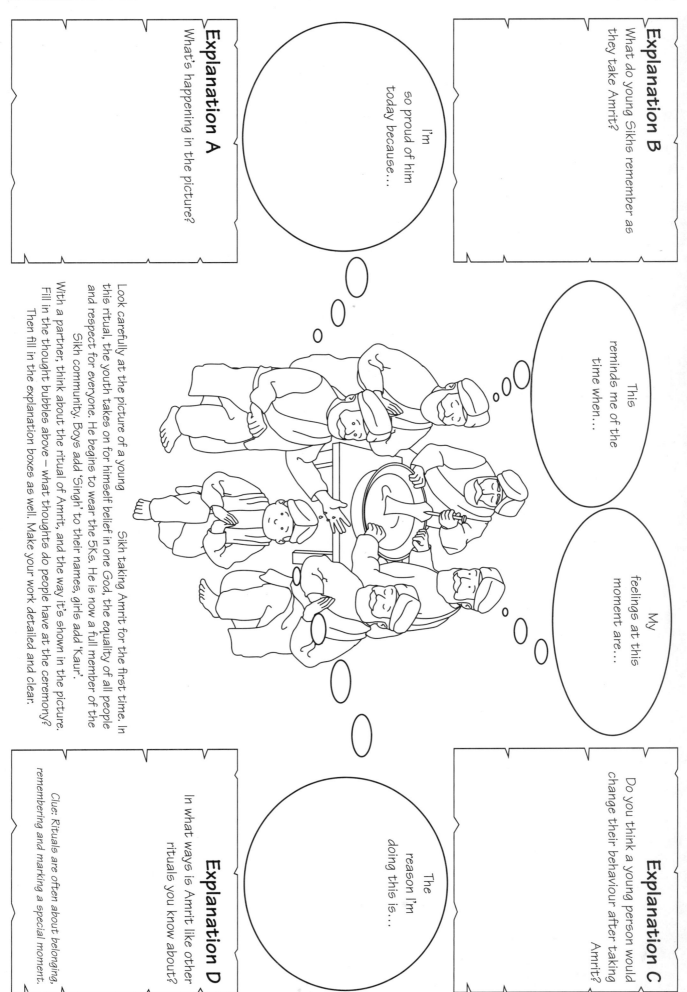

Look carefully at the picture of a young Sikh taking Amrit for the first time. In this ritual, the youth takes on for himself belief in one God, the equality of all people and respect for everyone. He begins to wear the 5Ks. He is now a full member of the Sikh community. Boys add 'Singh' to their names, girls add 'Kaur'.

With a partner, think about the ritual of Amrit, and the way it's shown in the picture. Fill in the thought bubbles above – what thoughts do people have at the ceremony? Then fill in the explanation boxes as well. Make your work detailed and clear.

Explanation C
Do you think a young person would change their behaviour after taking Amrit?

The reason I'm doing this is…

Explanation D
In what ways is Amrit like other rituals you know about?

Clue: Rituals are often about belonging, remembering and marking a special moment.